Hear Our Cries

Poems of Grief and Inspiration

June Keatts Wiggins

PROVIDENCE HOUSE PUBLISHERS
Franklin, Tennessee

Printed in the United States of America

04   03   02   01   00   1   2   3   4   5

Library of Congress Catalog Card Number: 00-100572

ISBN: 1-57736-175-X

Cover design by Gary Bozeman

A portion of the proceeds from the sale of this book will be offered to further the mission of the Tennessee Victims' Coalition and the Organized Victims of Violent Crimes.

PROVIDENCE HOUSE PUBLISHERS
238 Seaboard Lane • Franklin, Tennessee 37067
800-321-5692
www.providencehouse.com

TO

my precious son

Tim Wiggins

March 18, 1965, to February 19, 1989

and

in his memory

to all the parents

who have lost their precious children

for there is no grief like that of losing one's child

Contents

Foreword
viii

Preface
x

When Our Children Die
3

I'm Not Alone
6

If I Could Hear
8

Who's Going to Remember?
10

Twenty-three
12

Brother
16

Love Tim's Love
18

Until
19

Am I Dreaming?
20

Sharon
21

Little Girl
22

A Place Called Yesterday
24

Remember Me
28

A Year Ago
30

One Rose
34

Dear Tim
36

Imagine a Place
40

Memories of You
42

Forgive Me Tim
44

Your Love Is Alive
45

A Second Chance
46

Shattered Heart
48

Every Day
50

Tomorrow
52

Angels Don't Die
54

Tim
56

The Prayers
60

Our Friend
64

A Star
67

Heart of Tears
70

Blue Roses
74

It Could Have Been You in '89
78

Love Grows
82

The Mask
84

Behind the Smile
88

Teach Us
94

Glass Houses
98

The Gift
100

Distance Separates Us
104

Mother
106

If I Had Known Back Then
108

I'm Here
113

Whispers
116

Your Walk in Life
118

One
122

Heavenly Gates
125

Angel Tears
126

Heavy Load
128

A Man You Called Best Friend
130

A Mother for Life
132

My Angel
134

Christmas in Heaven
138

Tim and Tony
142

Hear Our Cries
145

About the Author
148

Foreword

IT HAS BEEN SEVERAL YEARS SINCE I FIRST MET JUNE WIGGINS. I was directing a support program for the bereaved called Courage For A New Day when June visited with a member of the monthly support group. After that she attended regularly. At some point, she brought me one of the poems that she had written. I found it to be deeply moving and expressive, and I communicated this to her. After reading more of her writings, I suggested to June that she consider publication so that a wider audience could have access to her reflections.

June is a very "simple person" in the best meaning of that phrase. Before the tragic death of her son Tim, she had never done writing of a sensitive and artistic nature and was not even aware she had the capability to do so. Tim had been the artist in the family, and it was his ability to communicate powerful emotions through writing that she greatly admired. After his death, she felt the need to put down her own feelings in words, and thus the poems in this book were born.

There are those of us who find writing to be a long and laborious process. This is not the case for June. Every one of the poems in this book was born in a moment of inspiration. They come suddenly in a burst of revelation, and June's task is to grab pen and paper and get the thoughts down before they escape. She believes that in some way the artistic soul of Tim is finding expression through her. As you ponder the words spoken here, you may sense the spiritual essence that has chosen June as the medium for its expression.

There are many reasons why I believe you may be helped through reflection on these writings. If you have not personally been touched by a painful death, you can let June teach you what deep grieving is like. For example, June captures the essence of the pervasive feelings of loneliness and longing found in mourning. "Spring, summer, fall, or winter. Seven days a week, all through the year, I miss you every day, because you are not here." She clearly communicates the desolation and emptiness of grief. "Imagine a place one morning where the sun doesn't shine, birds are not singing, and there is no end to time." Most of us have had some type of painful stab to our heart that enables us to identify with the powerful feelings expressed here.

If you are one of those whose "worst nightmare is coming true" because someone you love has died, you can find validation for what you are feeling in this book. I believe that this is true whatever the nature of your bereavement. It is almost magical how June can find that right combination of words to express the deepest and most complex feelings you may be experiencing. This will probably help you to develop a better understanding of what is happening to you and increase your courage to go on.

Whatever your situation, perhaps you will find certain phrases that will touch you and stay with you. Some that affect me deeply include: "If I could hear my mother call my name"; "There will be a tomorrow for you and me"; and "You are in my heart of tears."

In these reflections, you will find June's sense of the sacred. A profound spirituality pervades her writings. "Angels can't be seen with the eye, only felt with the heart and soul." She tells us of her faith that loved ones live beyond the grave and that we are not alone on our journey here.

June has often shared her gift of writing with others whose hearts are aching. The title of the book *Hear Our Cries* comes from a poem she wrote on behalf of all those who have been victimized. This book also includes the special tribute she wrote when my mother died. In this poem, she says that "a mother's love will never end." Over and over in these writings, we can see that her love for Tim has never ceased. I believe the most significant lesson she has learned from her suffering is that "Love doesn't die, love grows."

David H. Martin, Ph.D.
Professor and Clinical Psychologist
Tennessee State University

Preface

THESE POEMS OF GRIEF WERE INSPIRED BY THE DEATH OF MY son, Tim Wiggins, February 19, 1989, at the age of twenty-three. Since that time, I have worked constantly trying to prove who killed him, or to find out exactly what happened to him. I have been told many stories about his death and many lies.

Many people believe, as I do, that my son was murdered. These friends have supported me in my efforts to discover the truth, and for that I am eternally grateful. They continue to help me today. I pray that one day I will know what happened to Tim, for I will not stop until I have the truth.

There are many people who helped me while I was writing this book. I call them my "earth angels," because I believe that they were all sent by God.

Louanne Jennings's love and encouragement have helped me in so many ways. She is a true friend and a warm and wonderful person to know. She typed many of my poems, and for that I thank her.

Maxine Nabors is the best sister anyone could ask for. She's been there for me since Tim's death, helping and encouraging me in any way she could. She is a loving and wonderful sister and aunt, and I thank God for her. Thanks go to her also for typing some of my poems, even though she cried through every one of them.

Edith Hammons's love and hard work have done more than words can ever say to help me prove that Tim was murdered. She has spent hundreds of hours working to help me find the truth, and she has given me love and encouragement along the way. Her two sons are angels with Tim, and we've shared the same pain of losing them. My love goes to Edith and her family.

Kenneth Canady is the most honest man that I have ever met. He has helped me search for the truth, and he's a wonderful person to know. I thank God he is there for all those who need him.

Stephanie and Doug Lawson have always encouraged me to never quit trying to prove what happened to Tim. Doug is an angel now with his son and Tim, but even in his poor health he was a fighter for truth and justice. He inspired me, and he will be missed greatly.

Dr. Joanne Lagerson was an angel from the first day that I met her. Her love and encouragement have inspired me to go on. She is a great friend and a remarkable person to know, and a true blessing from God.

Dr. David Martin has inspired me to fight for truth and justice and to keep writing. His encouragement, wisdom, and friendship have been wonderful therapy for me and everyone who has met him. My love goes to him and his angel son in heaven.

I could not have done without Susan Oliver, a very special friend who helped me find Providence House Publishers. Her encouragement, care, and understanding were crucial in the publishing of this book, and for that I thank her.

Special thanks go to the staff of Providence House Publishers, who with their hard work and professionalism have helped make this book a reality.

Charity Bernath, who is like a daughter to me, would have made the perfect sister for Tim, though she never knew him. She provided much love and encouragement, and also typed several poems. I treasure her friendship, and thank her for all of her many gifts.

My thanks also go to Joy King, who has been my "Angel in Disguise." She knew and loved Tim, and her love and hard work have been a great help to me in my search for truth. She has also typed many poems, and her dedication helped make this book possible.

Many thanks go to Jan Mumford, who feels that Tim is now her guardian angel. She has done so much to help me that will never be forgotten, and I thank God for blessing me with her loving friendship.

My love goes to Essie Beller, who adopted my family and we her. Essie never knew Tim in life, but loves him and our family now with all her heart. If Tim could have chosen his grandparents, I know it would have been Essie and her husband, Kenneth. Tim and Kenneth became angels the same year, and I know that Kenneth is Tim's grandfather up in heaven. Essie's love has been my greatest inspiration and encouragement. God let us meet, and now we walk together.

Many thanks go to my son Jason Wiggins, who has inspired me to keep writing and to go on with my life to do the things that Tim would have wanted. Years ago, he was the answer to Tim's prayers and one of Tim's greatest joys in life. I thank God every day that I have him because I could not go on without him.

My love also goes to my husband, Tom Wiggins, whose love, support, patience, and understanding helped make this book of poems possible. We have traveled a long, hard journey together, with many tears, pain, and heartaches along the way. Tom now knows that I will never give up trying to prove what happened to our son and understands what I have to do, for there is no greater love on this earth than a mother's.

To everyone I haven't mentioned, you know who you are. I thank all of my friends and Tim's friends for all of the love and help that you have given to me, especially your support in helping me find the truth and justice that Tim deserves, and I pray that you will continue to help me search. Your faith in Tim and love for him and my family bless us every day. We love you all.

I pray that everyone who reads this book of poems will keep us in their prayers. There are secret angels out there helping us all.

Hear
Our
Cries

When Our Children Die

IN MEMORY OF MY SON TIM WIGGINS
MY BROTHER WILLIAM KEATTS
TONY BENTLEY
BOBBY HALE
JOE HAMMONS
MIKE HAMMONS
BOBBY HICKMAN
DOUG LAWSON JR.
MIKE SIMPKINS
AND TO ALL THE OTHER SONS AND DAUGHTERS WHO HAVE DIED
AND THEIR PARENTS

When our children die
All we can do is pray to God and cry,
And ask why not us instead of them.
When our children die we keep asking ourselves,
Why did they go and leave a hole in our hearts
That keeps tearing us apart, that can never be repaired,
Till the end of time?

When our children die,
Where we had love now there is pain,
And loneliness will always remain.
Nothing will ever be the same.
When our children die, we die too.

Oh, how we love and miss you, to see your face
And touch your hands,
Would mean so much to us Moms and Dads.

When our children die
They die by guns, cars, drugs, alcohol,
Sickness, and more.

They were precious daughters and sons,
What more could any parent ask for?
We cry and say we can't take it anymore.
For them to be with us once more
We would all give our lives,
When our children die.

There will never be any more to take their place
And till the end of time
All our hearts will break.

April 24, 1990

I'm Not Alone

IN MEMORY OF WILLIAM KEATTS
MARCH 8, 1938, TO AUGUST 8, 1988

"I'm going with Jesus.
It won't be long,
I'm going with Jesus,
And I'm not alone."

As he lay dying in his bed, the preachers gathered
And they touched his hands.
Then they said, "If you believe in God, My Son,
He'll forgive the sins that you've done."
Little did they know he had relived his life,
And through Jesus, was sanctified.

Our brother died that very day,
And as they bowed their heads to pray,
They heard him say, "I'm going with Jesus. It won't be long,
I'm going with Jesus, and I'm not alone."

As they said good-bye,
He closed his eyes, with Jesus standing,
Standing by his side.
They'll never forget what they saw that day
As Jesus took him home to stay.

"I'm going with Jesus, finally going home,
I'm going with Jesus,
And I'm not alone."

If I Could Hear

If I could hear my Mother call my name,
If I could hear her tender voice so dear,
So glad I would be, it would mean a lot to me,
If I could hear my mother call my name.

When we were little children playing in the yard,
We used to hear her calling to come on inside,
We pretended we didn't hear,
We didn't want to go,
But if I could hear her calling now,
I would gladly go.

If I could hear my Mother call my name,
If I could hear her tender voice so dear,
So glad I would be, it would mean a lot to me,
If I could hear my mother call my name.

She went to be with Brother,
They're waiting there for me,
They're waiting up in Heaven
So very patiently.
If I could hear her calling now
I would gladly go.

If I could hear my Mother call my name,
If I could hear her tender voice so dear,
So glad I would be, it would mean a lot to me,
If I could hear my mother call my name.

October 23, 1988

Who's Going to Remember?

Who's going to remember?
Who's going to know?
Just a name carved on a stone.

They were someone's fathers,
Someone's mothers, someone's children,
Husbands or wives,
But who's going to remember?
Who's going to know?
Just a name carved on a stone.

They once had families,
They once had wives,
They once had someone to share their lives.
They once were happy, they once were sad,
But who's going to remember?
Who's going to know?
Just a name carved on a stone.

A few years later, when we're gone,
Who's going to remember?
Who's going to know?
Just a name carved on a stone.

We were someone's fathers,
Someone's mothers, someone's children,
Husbands, or wives,
But who's going to remember?
Who's going to know?
Just a name carved on a stone.

December 7, 1988

Twenty-three

A young man died at twenty-three,
All he left behind were us three,
To some he's not even a memory,
Just a young man to be talked about.
An angel he never claimed to be,
He was innocent he swore to me.
All he ever wanted was to be free.
But they never wanted that to be.
All we have now is his memory.
He was only twenty-three.

They said he took his life that February day,
But who really killed him, I want to say.
The ones who lied,
The ones who said bad things about him,
The ones who didn't believe him,
Or the ones who let him down when he depended on them.
All he left were us three and his memory,
He was only twenty-three.

They said a grief-stricken mother
Doesn't know what she's talking about,
But next time you could be that mother
They are talking about.

People don't realize the harm that was done.
They should check their conscience, if they have one.
To see what could have been done
To save a young man, from being just a memory
At twenty-three.

But God blessed us,
He was our son.
All he left behind were us three, and his memory,
He was only twenty-three.

He can't be hurt anymore
By things that are said and done.
God knows the truth and
We're glad he's safe and free.

All he left behind were us three, and a memory,
He was only twenty-three,
And very precious to us three.

Brother

Brother, why did you have to go,
And leave me here all alone?
I loved you, didn't you see?
You meant the whole, wide world to me.

I'll love you till eternity, brother,
Why did you die?
I'd still be standing by your side.

They said you did some things
You did not do.
God knows how they lied on you.
It made you cry and made you blue,
You were innocent.
They did not see you meant the whole, wide world to me.
Brother, why did you have to go,
And leave me here all alone?

Brother, you were good,
They didn't want to see.
They only brought you pain and misery.
You only wanted to be free.
They said that could never be.
You were only twenty-three . . .

Now way down deep inside I cry.
Why did you have to die,
And leave me here all alone?
I loved you, didn't you see?
You meant the whole, wide world to me.

I'll love you till the day I die.
Will this pain ever subside,
And someday set me free?
Brother, why did you have to die?
I'd still be standing by your side.
Why did you have to go,
And leave me here alone?

February 19, 1989

Love Tim's Love

After I'm gone,
Give what's left of me away.
To young people who need love,
And remind you of me.
To old people who are lonely,
And pray for some company.

Cry for your brothers, and sisters,
Neighbors, and friends, who also
Know the pain within.

When you need and want me,
Put your arms around someone else,
And give to them what you want to give to me.
I want to leave something in this world,
That money can't buy.
That might someday help you in time.
Look for me in people I've known,
Or loved, and give me away, because that's love.

The best way I know to let me live is to give.
You will love me most by loving someone else,
And by giving me away a little every day.

January 18, 1990

Until

FOR THE FAMILY OF DOUG LAWSON JR.

Don't know what we'll do when the sun comes up each day.

Oh how we miss you and think about you every day.

Until we see your face again, and hear you call our names.

Greatly you were loved, and now our life is incomplete.

Life without you will never be the same.

All of us now have to live with this pain.

Wanting to see you when we hear your name.

Son, you were a joy and comfort to us all.

On our minds you will always remain.

Now you're gone and only God knows the pain.

Just waiting to see you again so our hearts can mend.

Right now we love you and pray you are safe

Until we're all together again.

April 14, 1990

Am I Dreaming?

When I fell asleep last night, I prayed to God to hold you tight,
I closed my eyes, I saw the light,
Is this real or am I dreaming?

I saw a face and eyes so blue, with arms outstretched and
Tears running down our faces,
When you said, "Oh, how I love and miss you, I want to talk to you."
Then I knew it was really you,
Is this real or am I dreaming?

You sat me down and took my hand, I saw a smile upon your face.
You said, "Life doesn't end, I watch over you,
Family, and friends just until we meet again."
Is this real or am I dreaming?

You said, "Life is sometimes short and full of pain,
Where nothing remains the same,
Things that happen in life are so insignificant
Compared to life for eternity, it is so different."
Is this real or am I dreaming?

You said, "I wanted you to know I'm safe and happy."
You kissed my cheek and said, "I have to go, love never dies,
I'll always be right by your side,
This is from God and me,
We'll be together again for all eternity."

I awake and ask,
Is this real or am I dreaming?

July 30, 1990

Sharon

To Mr. and Mrs. Mayberry

S She was a little girl
God gave us to hold,
A lot more precious
Than silver or gold.
H Her ways were so good,
Sweet and kind.
When God gave her to us,
I thought she would be mine.
A As time went on, I did not see,
She was his, and not mine.
I could have her only
A very short time.
R Really God loved her more, you see,
And when it was time,
He would give her back to me.
Only love is something,
O That death cannot part.
Our precious little girl,
That God gave us,
Is still in our hearts.
N Never will we part,
When we meet again,
That precious little girl,
God gave us to hold,
A lot more precious
Than silver and gold.
Will always be mine,
She was his for only
A very short time.

July 30, 1990

Little Girl

WITH LOVE TO AARON AND JEANNE LITTON
AND THEIR UNBORN CHILD
FROM TIM AND MIKE

Little Girl, you haven't been born yet,
So we don't know your name,
If you were a boy, you would be named Timothy Michael
And leave out the Wayne.
You'll always be so precious to us,
If you were a boy you would be named after us.

We'll watch out after you, from high up above,
And make sure we send you all our love.
We'll never meet you, while you're here on this earth,
But you'll know who we are,
We'll shine over you like a big bright star.

Little girl we don't know your name,
But we love you just the same,
You'll always be so precious to us,
Had you been a boy you would be named after us.

We can't be there to help you along,
But we want you to know you'll never be alone.
If we were there, we could hold you in our arms,
And tell you how precious you are.
We'll have to be satisfied to love you from afar.

We'll watch over you and keep you safe,
No one else could take your place,
And one day we'll meet you in a special place. . . .

November 11, 1990

A Place Called Yesterday

If I could go back to yesterday, I could keep you safe.
I could tell you no one else could ever take your place.
I could tell you how proud of you I was,
I would try to make you happy
And feel loved, and not out of place,
I would be so happy to see your face.

I would hold you tight, and never let you go,
I could finally tell you how much I love you.
All the things I could never tell you before,
I could make up for the things that lay in store.

I would pray to God every day not to let anyone hurt you,
To let you have a good and happy life,
To find peace and love,
The things you searched for inside all your life.

I could hold you in my arms and tell you how precious you are,
Say all the things I need to say,
And do the things I needed to do for you.
If I could go back to yesterday,
I never would have lost you.

My heart would be happy inside, I would never have to face
Another day without you by my side.
If I could go back to yesterday,
I could protect you from the hurt and pain,
Where we could stay there,
Where all remains the same.

If I could go back to yesterday, you never would have cried.
If I could go back to yesterday, you never would have died,
And we never would have to say good-bye.

I could wipe out all your fears and give you hope,
And dry your tears.
If I could go back to yesterday,
I wouldn't have to face the pain, hurt, and hopelessness
I feel today.
If I could go back to yesterday,
You would be back there, a place in time,
Called yesterday. . . .

January 10, 1991

Remember Me

When I'm gone don't cry for me,
For that would only bring me more pain and misery.
Be happy, and remember the memories.

Remember the good things I tried to do, and not the bad.
Remember the happy things I said, and not the sad.

Remember the things that made me happy,
The things I loved to do,
But most of all remember, "I love all of you."

Remember the sadness, the pain, and don't cry for me,
For none remains.
Remember me laughing, and not crying,
Remember me as I was, not as I am now,
And try to be proud.

When I'm not here, I'll be with my Tim
And the others that I love, and long to see.
You'll still have our love and all the
Memories.

So miss me if you must, and don't be sorry,
Talk of me, and be happy.
Bring a bouquet of flowers when you can,
But most of all remember, I love you and don't be sad.

The ones we leave behind hurt and suffer more
Than those who are at rest.
So don't cry for me, just think of
"Peace and Happiness."

February 24, 1991

A Year Ago

I went to bed last night,
I said a prayer, and turned out the lights.

It was the time I always talked to you.

It will be a year ago tomorrow
Since you died, it's been so lonely
Without you, such a long time.
We miss the smile upon your face,
Nothing else could take its place.

I won't be able to get through the day tomorrow,
Unless I know you're safe and happy,
That I'll see you again in a better place.

Do something to let me know it's from you,
And then I'll be able to get through.

Morning came, I heard you say,
"It has been a year ago today, look outside and you will see."
The prettiest heart-shaped balloon,
That could be found, hung in your tree so big and proud.
Written there, "You are so special to me."

Pink, blue ribbons, hearts and all.
So beautiful, so high above the ground,
I knew my prayers had been found.

Fall came, the leaves were gone,
But the balloon still hung on strong.

Then one day, it was not there,
The wind had blown throughout the night
And my balloon was not in sight.

Left hanging on a smaller tree,
Nothing blew now, but just a small breeze.
I could reach up with so little ease, and get my balloon
From the smaller tree.

It hangs on the wall in your room now, a reminder
That you're happy, safe, and free.
A gift from my son to me.

May 12, 1991

One Rose

I awoke one cold and frosty morning,
It was the month of December, and trying to snow.
Wanting to see you, I knew I had a long way to go.

It had been so long since I saw you,
I just had to make the drive,
So I could be close at your side.

I'll take you your favorite flowers,
I said to myself.
If it were summer I would pick you a big bunch,
But all I have is one red rose, to take you.
I know you'll understand,
It's winter, cold, dreary, and very bad.

You're on a hill where the cold wind blows,
Waiting there to see me, just like I knew you would be.

If I could hold you in my arms one more time,
To say I love you, to know you are safe,
To see your face.

If only I could take your place, or tell you,
I'm sorry for all my mistakes.
I cried and placed the rose upon your stone,
And went on home, so all alone.

I awoke one cold and frosty morning,
Rushing outside, wanting to find you there.
What I saw wasn't you.

A rose bush all dead and brown,
Not one green leaf could be found,
But in the middle was one red rose,
And then I knew, it was for me,
With love from you.

May 12, 1991

Dear Tim

I'm writing you this letter,
It's been so long since you went away,
I pray for you and long to see you, each and every day.
You never got to say good-bye to us that day,
I wish I could have seen you one last time, but we both know,
We could never have said good-bye.

I'm writing you this letter, if you see it you'll know,
Just how sad we are and so alone.
We didn't say the things we wanted to say before you went away,
If we had the chance this is what we would say to you today.

That we loved you more than we ever let you know,
That we needed you more than you were ever told,
That we made mistakes,
That you had a heart of gold,
That you were always there when I cried,
I thought you would always be,
That we need you so very much,
How you always put us first,
That you were good, hardworking, honest, and kind.
All of this you could never see,
I've made too many mistakes you would say to me.

If you could be here today, it would mean the world to us,
If you could be here today, it would stop the hurt and pain,
If we could have you back with us,
We would never ask for anything.

If we could have one more chance to make up to you
For the things we did not do,
So much we should have said and done for you.
All of our chances now are gone,
It's too late to let you know how we feel,
That without you, there is a void as big as the world
That will never be filled.

I'm writing you this letter and pray to God to let you read,
That the ones who lied and hurt you will see,
And that their conscience will never be free,
For what they did to you and me.
For the young life that was taken away,
The hopes and dreams all shattered to dust,
Just how precious you were to us.
How you deserved so much
But got so little,
How you were used and tossed aside,
How you never got to say good-bye.
How we couldn't see you one last time,
How you should have lived and not died. . . .

Dear Tim, I'm writing this letter so all can see . . .
And pray to God to let you read it.

Always and Forever,
Mom

September 23, 1991

Imagine a Place

Imagine a place one morning
Where the sun doesn't shine,
Birds are not singing,
And there is no end to time.
The grass has turned brown,
All the leaves have fallen to the ground.

Imagine there are no flowers that bloom
Or rivers that flow,
No stars at night or moon aglow.
No music, no singing, a place that's so dark
Where you're all alone.

Imagine a place where time stands still
Because tomorrow is just too hard to fill.
Where no one would want to live.
No joy or smiling faces. No laughter,
Only sorrow and pain,
Where nothing will ever be the same.

Imagine there's no rain, nothing grows.
All withers and dies.
Where all the people cry,
Where they will never understand,
Why it had to happen like this.

Imagine a place where you can't see your child's face,
Hold him in your arms, feel his embrace,
Or tell him you love him ever again.
Or see him get married, or hold his child,
Or see him grow old.

Imagine a place where you'll never want to go,
Imagine your worst nightmares coming true,
This is our world without you.
This is where we live now.

Imagine a place.

December 3, 1991

Memories of You

In my memory I can see that little
White-headed, blue-eyed boy,
Who brought me flowers he picked from the yard.
He knocked upon my door.
He said I love you this much and more.

In my memories I can see a young boy,
I can see his smile,
I can hear his laughter,
I can see his face so clear,
I can see the way he walked and the wave of his hand.
In my memories I can hear
His words of love and comfort,
I can see his heart is pure.

In my memories I go to see him often,
It's where he'll always have to be,
And when I need him,
I'll go there,
But that's not fair.

As a young man I can see his hurt and feel his pain.
I see his love and
In my memories he will always be the same,
Because he never got the chance to grow old.
In my memories he will never be old. . . .

May 10, 1992

Forgive Me Tim

I tried so hard to clear your name,
And have the proof to do it,
But they don't care,
Life goes on for them, but not for you or us.

You tried so hard to do your best,
Now I've done my best.
So, Tim, please forgive me
For I have failed you, and
You will never rest.

I'm not quitting, Tim, I just need to rest awhile,
I'm so tired and weary.
I'll always love you with all my heart and
Pray one day soon people will love enough
To help you and me.
To come forward and
Help me prove who murdered you.
To care enough that you were innocent
For the crimes you were charged with,
To clear your name.

One day soon, Tim, you can rest. . . .

I love and miss you forever,
Mom

May 10, 1992

Your Love Is Alive

Tim, your love is alive.
As I walk through this world without you,
I wonder where you are.
I wonder if you see us even from afar.
When I'm sad and lonely, I feel your presence near.
I can almost see you and know you are here.

Your love is alive in my memories,
I see the smile so dear,
I hear your voice so clear.
I see the way you walked,
The things you left behind,
I know you are here.

Your love is alive,
When I remember the thoughtful things
You said and did,
For as long as we live,
Your love will always be here.

May 26, 1992

A Second Chance

I go to see you, I always will,
There's a hole in my heart that needs to be filled.
I talk to you so you'll know just how I feel,
I love you, and miss you, and God knows, I always will.

    The pain in my heart is too hard to bear.
    For a second chance, oh, what I would give,
    As I ask God, why you did not live.

My tears, they fall upon the ground
And form a puddle, small and round,
But my peace cannot be found.

As I sat upon the ground, I heard a noise,
I saw a light that was so big and very bright.
An old man stood there looking down.
A long white robe, sandals on his feet,
A smile on his face, tears on his cheeks.
"I'm here my child," he said to me.
"Your father sees all your pain and misery,
He knows your heart and will set you free."

"The second chance you ask for will be given to you in time,
The son who was taken from you will be given back to you.
The pain in your heart will be healed.
The tears in your eyes will be dry.
The hole in your heart will be filled,
And your peace will be found.
Your son is not gone, God has just taken him home."

December 19, 1992

Shattered Heart

This shattered heart will never heal,
Tho' they say it always will.
All shattered to pieces,
All broken in two,
This shattered heart is because I've lost you.

Shattered, broken, so many pieces,
Hardly any life.
No will to live.
All black and blue, all torn apart.
A shattered heart is hard to heal,
When you know it never will.

Once shattered, bruised, broken in two,
No one can fix it,
Except you.

This shattered heart will be put back together,
The bruises all healed,
The pain will be gone, and life restored,
When I see you
And we are together once more.

January 8, 1993

Every Day

It's not your birthday, Christmas, or Easter,
Or the day you died,
But I miss you hundreds of times,
Every day since you were taken away.

Spring, summer, fall, or winter.
Seven days a week,
All through the year,
I miss you every day,
Because you are not here.

First thing every morning, I miss your hellos.
Last thing at night I miss you saying,
"Good night, sleep tight."

It has been four long years
Since you went away,
And I miss you more today
Than yesterday.

For the rest of my life,
Every day of the year,
I will miss you.
Until we meet again,
Then you can dry all my tears.

January 8, 1993

Tomorrow

There will be a tomorrow for you and me,
A time and a place for us to be.
For all we have now is the hurt, pain,
And your memories.
Tomorrow the truth will be told and
You will have your peace and rest,
For you deserve the very best.

Tomorrow the ones who destroyed you
Will be punished for what they did to you.
Tomorrow the ones who think you are forgotten
Will see they are wrong.
Your truth and your memory still live on.

Tomorrow they will know your pain,
How it feels to be destroyed, and
What they did to you was very wrong.
For God knows the truth.
It can only be hidden for so long.

You were good, kind, and giving
With a very soft heart.
You were not perfect, no one is,
You died for what you knew,
Not for what you did.

But tomorrow you will live,
For God in heaven said you will.

There will be a tomorrow for you and me,
A place and time for us to be
Where we will have peace and rest
For all eternity.

The ones who destroyed you
Will be punished for all to see,
But for now they are free.
God never wanted that to be.

January 21, 1993

Angels Don't Die

You left us behind the day you were taken away,
The pain in our hearts just won't go away.
We love you and miss you more today
Than we did yesterday.
We feel your presence and love every day.
The memories of you are stronger each day.

Angels don't die,
They are just away, and
Will return to you
When you need them most.

You watch over us and keep us safe,
Wherever we are, you are with us.
We know you are with us,
We feel you so close,
We will be together again in a better place.

Angels don't die,
They watch over you day and night,
And will return to you
When you need them most.
They have more important things to do,
Then they will be returned to me and you.

Angels can't be seen with the eye,
Only felt with the heart and soul.
When you have an angel,
You will never be alone.

July 6, 1993

Tim

The time we spent together since I was eighteen,
Sometimes it seemed that all I had was you and me.
The times were hard, and sometimes bad,
But I tried to make do with what I had.

I wasn't the best, though I tried to be,
So young and restless, wanting to be free.
I had a son, so that could not be.
An hour or so, just to be alone,
What would I give, though it wasn't to be.

In the twenty years we spent together,
We fought, laughed, loved each other, and cried,
But I didn't mind.
I thought I would always have you,
And you would always be mine.
When I was that young girl of eighteen,
I thought we had lots of time.

Little did I know it was not to be.
At the young age of twenty-three,
You were taken from me.
Now I cry, I don't want to be free,
Though it was meant to be.

Memories of you are all I have left now.
I spend hours and hours just thinking of you.
Just wishing I could go back, and hold you tight.
Oh, what I would give for an hour or two
Just to spend them with you,
Though it wasn't meant to be.
Now I cry and don't want to be free,
For all I had back then was
You and me.

October 25, 1993

The Prayers

Jason, twenty-one years ago,
God answered Tim's prayer,
To have a little brother he could call his own, to love and share.
Someone to be with, so he would never be alone.
A brother he could talk to, be proud of,
So God sent him you, twenty-one years ago.

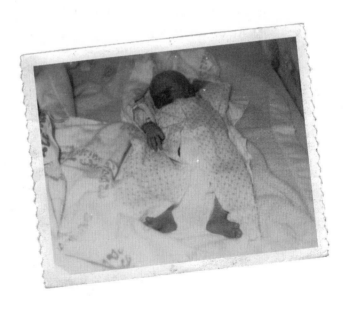

You were his pride, he was so proud of you.
He loved you with all his heart.
He knew you would do great things right from the start,
And from the beginning, you had a place in his heart.

He thought he would always be there
To help take care of you.
If he could be here now, how proud he would be,
But he was killed at twenty-three.

He is not here for your birthday, Jason,
But I hope you feel his spirit and love.
You were the only prayer
He ever asked for himself from God up above.
He watches over you and keeps you safe.
And wants you to know, you will always be loved.
You are his special prayer, his only brother,
His brother to love.

So make him proud in the years to come.
Do the things he said he would do.
He thought it was the greatest thing in the world
To have a little brother like you.
You were his prayer and ours, too.

Have a wonderful birthday, Jason, and a happy one, too.
Love from your brother and us, too.

Love you forever,
Tim, Mom, and Dad

November 11, 1993

Our Friend

FOR EDITH, ON HER BIRTHDAY
FROM ESSIE BELLER, MR. AND MRS. DOUG LAWSON,
JAN MUMFORD, JUNE WIGGINS, AND ALL THE OTHER VICTIMS
SHE HAS HELPED IN LIFE

Edith,
God made you special,
And we know you are.
You lead the way.
You are our shining star.

You are there in our sorrows,
You feel the pain in our hearts.
You have always been there to love us,
And to guide our way.
On our dark and dreary days,
You are our shoulder to cry on.
You have always had the time to listen to us,
To help us get through.
If we searched the whole world over,
We would never find a friend like you.

God had a plan for us to meet.
He knew we would need you,
That you would always be there to love us
And help us along the way.
To share our pain,
For we would never be the same.
He knew you had been there,
Where we are now,
That is why you are so special,
Our shining star.

If we searched the whole world over,
We would never find a friend like you.
We love you.
 God knew what he was doing,
  When he sent us to you.
   He always has a plan to help us, when he can.

We love you, Happy Birthday!

November 24, 1993

A Star

There is a star at night,
That shines so big and very bright.
On clear and cloudy nights,
It's right there to guide our way,
Each and every night.
To let us know you are watching over us,
That is your way to let us see that you love us.
To give us hope,
In that star we see at night,
That shines so big and very bright.

I never saw it before you were killed.
Then I saw it one cold and cloudy night.
It has been there ever since.
A sign to me, it seemed, from up above,
From God, with all your love,
In that star we see at night.

Your body was killed, but your spirit lives,
And I know it always will.
Your love, faith, and hope are there for all to see,
In a star that shines at night,
So big and very bright,
On clear and cloudy nights.

Sometimes it twinkles,
Sometimes it glows.
When I look in the sky at night,
I know we will never be alone.
Your spirit shines from up above
To let us know we will always be loved.

January 13, 1994

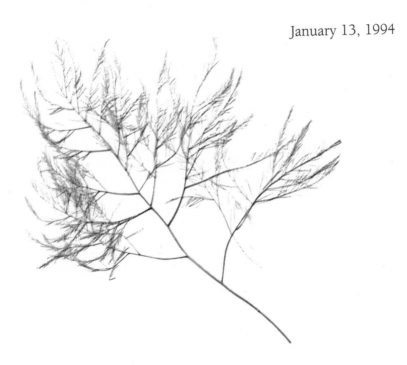

Heart of Tears

A heart of tears can't be seen or felt by others.
The tears flow all the time.
There is never an end.
Your heart is full, you almost drown.
It is full of pain and misery.
You walk around, but no one sees.
No one hears a heart of tears.

A heart of tears is never dry.
It is broken in two, all black and blue
And very bruised.
The worst pain that's ever been felt.
It is with you night and day,
Every day of the year.

A heart of tears will never heal,
When a child of yours has been killed.
No one sees, no one hears a heart of tears.

An empty space within your heart,
All full of tears that nothing can fill.
The pain is so deep, there is no end.
Like a bottomless pit that is long and wide,
It is all in there, the hurt, sorrow,
Not ever getting to see you again.
A heart like this can never mend.
No amount of time or years
Will ever heal a heart of tears.

I love you, son, more today than yesterday.
I miss you more, not less every day.
I can't see you or hear your voice ever again,
But you are in my heart of tears.

Pray that this won't ever happen to you,
That you won't be like me.
I pray that your child doesn't have to live
In a heart of tears.

Blue Roses

It was time for me to visit you,
And leave some flowers by the stone at your head.
It's been five years now since you were taken away from me,
I miss you so much, seems like only yesterday.
The pain is just as bad today
As the day you died.
All I can do now is cry
And ask, why?

I stopped at a little flower shop along the road,
To buy your flowers,
I hadn't seen this one here before.
I must have missed it the other times I had driven by.
I told the little old man, so kind he seemed,
I need some roses to take to my son.

There were tears in his eyes,
And I could see the pain
As he touched my hand.
It was as if he knew.

He said, "I'm sorry about your son,
All we have left in roses are blue.
They don't sell very good, though,
All the ones that were sold were brought back.
They ruined a wedding, scared a new mother and baby,
And spoiled a birthday,
But they might be just right for your son."

I bought the roses and hurried along.
I placed them with love by the stone at your head.
The roses seemed to come alive,
And begin to cry.
There were tears on the roses.
Now I knew why they were blue,
And were wrong for others,
But just right for you.

I went on back thinking of the little old man.
I wanted to stop and tell him about the roses.
I looked and looked,
But there was no sign of him or the flower shop.
I wanted to tell him the roses were for you,
And would not be brought back.
I've gone down that road many times since,
But never saw the little old man again.
Then I knew the blue roses were heaven-sent just for you,
And they cry for you just like I do.

January 13, 1994

It Could Have Been You in '89

It could have been you who was accused
Of things you did not do.
It could have been you who died that February day
All alone in such a terrible way.
So young, so trusting, so full of life.
Not knowing what was in store.
It could have been you and then
You wouldn't want it to happen anymore.

It could have been you who searched
For the truth the last five years,
Who was lied to, right from the start,
Whose tears still fall.
It could have been your husband,
Brother, or child, like mine,
There were plenty of deaths in '89.

It could have been you they wouldn't take
A polygraph test for
Or give you any proof of what happened.
It could have been your son that died, not mine,
On that day in '89.
So in August when the time is right
Remember what I am saying . . . it could have been you,
Your husband, brother, or child, like mine,
There were plenty of deaths in '89.

And your heart would be breaking, like mine,
Till the end of time.
Remember Tim and don't let it happen anymore.
Search your heart before you sign
Or yours will break, like mine,
Till the end of time.

July 6, 1994

Love Grows

I try to make them understand.
I try to let them know.
Love doesn't die, love grows.
Day after day, year after year
It gets stronger and stronger.
Nothing can touch it.
Nothing can make it go away.
Love gets stronger each and every day.
The day you died your love for us didn't die.
It's still there for us to feel.
You left us love, it was all you had to give.
The greatest gift of all,
For love never dies, it always lives
And grows day after day, year after year.
They don't understand, they don't know.
Our love for you still grows.
It's all we have to give you now
Until we meet again.
Nothing can touch it.
Nothing can make it go away.

Our love gets stronger, our love still grows
Day after day, year after year.
It gets stronger every day.
Our love for you will grow until the day we die
No matter how many years we live
Without you as time goes by.
You were our child and our love for you will never die.
They think because you're not here
That we loved you in the past.
They don't know love still grows.
God waters it each and every day
For it was all you had to leave us.
And love will always grow
Day after day, year after year
Until we meet our child again.
Love is a gift that lasts forever.
The greatest gift of all.
Nothing can touch it.
Nothing can make it go away.
Love grows.

November 22, 1994

The Mask

The mask we all wear every day hides
All the heartache, hurt, pain, hate and love that no one knows.
Take the mask away, we are afraid of what people would see,
For our deepest, darkest secrets would be known.
The things we never told anyone would all be heard.
The hurt, the pain we feel would all be known,
The hate all would see, and the love would all be felt.

People wear all kinds of masks.
Some show no hurt or pain,
For they have suffered too much in the past to let it show.
Some have a pure heart where so much love grows,
But they are afraid to let it show,
It was crushed and broken so many times
Back down that road.
Some pretend to be so tough and not to care,
But their soft hearts are breaking inside and
Their hearts cry out,
All alone behind that mask they wear every day.

Other people wear masks that show so much love,
But hate hides within.
Some show friendship and compassion, but there is none inside.
Some show pain and hurt that is all pretend.
Some look nice and sweet, but inside are hard and mean.
They hide their lies, for they know not the truth.
They hurt others, but no one sees.
The masks hide all.
From the outside we are so proud of them.
Pull away the masks
Then all would see underneath
The things they hide away so very neatly.
They pretend they are something they are not,
And fool everyone behind that mask they wear every day.

None were born with masks,
They grew them along the way.
The good out of their pain and hurt,
The bad out of their hate.
It only matters to them what people think.

God knows what lies behind the masks
That no one sees,
And one day the masks will have to come off
And they will be judged for what is hidden there,
Not for what the people see.

January 3, 1995

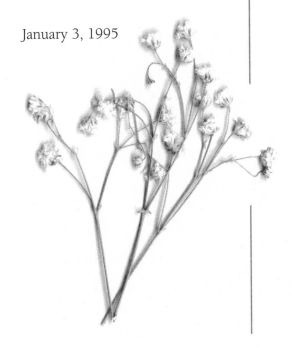

Behind the Smile

He was a young man of twenty-three.
Brown hair, blue eyes, a smile for all to see.
A man outside, a child to him and me.
He looked so worldly and so wise,
But really was just a child inside.
Pretending to be tough, but so soft and tender.
He hid his hurt and pain behind a smile.

He loved with all his heart and soul.
He was hurt so many times
By the ones he loved and cared about.
He was put down, made fun of, and lied about.
He could never find the true love
He searched for all his life,
And he hid his hurt and pain behind the smile.

He was a good person,
Sweet and kind,
A man outside, a child inside,
He tried so hard to make us happy,
To do what was right,
To make us proud,
But nothing he did was ever good enough,
So he hid his hurt and pain behind the smile.

He's gone now, it seems like forever,
He got no praise here on earth,
But a big reward up in heaven.
He stills tries to make us happy,
And shows his love for us every day.
He watches over us and keeps us safe.
His love was so strong it could never leave us.
A man outside, a child to him and me.

I look at his picture every day now.
He has made us happy and so very proud.
I see the twinkle in his eyes of blue,
The love on his face,
And the happiness behind his smile.

He got no praise while here on earth,
For his reward was waiting up in heaven,
And the smile on his face is very real.
Praise here on earth is worthless,
But the rewards up in heaven are forever.

January 4, 1995

Teach Us

Jehovah God,
Each and every day, we face despair,
Painful beyond words,
For our precious child was taken away from us,
All at once.
At such a young and tender stage of life,
It seems he was much too young to die,
For we needed him so very much.
Teach us how to live without our child.

Sometimes we just can't accept it,
And it doesn't seem real.
Sometimes we think it's a bad nightmare
And that we'll wake up to find that it is not true.
It hurts so much to know that we are awake
And wishing it were a nightmare.
Teach us how to live with the awful truth.

We ask you to comfort us throughout our lives.
We need you so much to learn how to survive without our child.
Death is so painful, the pain never ends.
We need you each and every day all through the coming years.
We ask you never to leave us alone,
For we could never make it on our own.

The horror and pain of death are too much to accept all at once.
To lose a child will take a lifetime.
Each and every day we remember special days
And memories from the past
That still live within our broken hearts.

Jehovah God,
A child is such a precious thing to lose.
We need you to teach us how to survive for the rest of our lives.
Help us to go on,
For it is such a long, hard road without our child.

Teach us how to be happy again, even for a little while.
Teach us how to forget, if only for one moment,
Without the awful pain that is in our hearts.
Teach us to laugh again and dry our tears,
But most of all, teach us how to live again without our child.

January 21, 1995

Glass Houses

People who live in glass houses usually holler the loudest.
They think that they're so perfect,
That they never did anything.
But be careful of stones that you throw.

They think that they are much better than all of the others.
That what they did was not wrong.
People in glass houses are usually the proudest,
So be careful of stones that you throw.

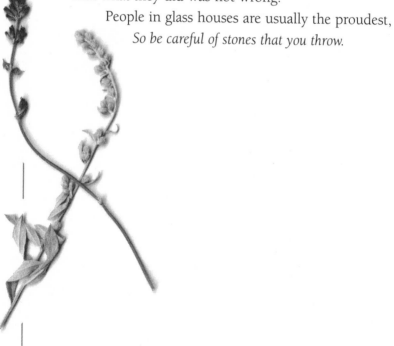

Glass houses can shatter, and then it won't matter.
They will see you're not perfect and that it all was for nothing.
They will see you are not better than all of the others,
And what you did was wrong.
So be careful of stones that you throw.

People who live in glass houses will no longer be prouder,
They will be ashamed of the truth.
Glass houses can shatter, and then it won't matter.
So be careful of stones that you throw.

January 21, 1995

The Gift

Lord, you gave me a gift, when I was only a young girl,
Much too young to appreciate such a gift.
I thought the gift you gave me would last a lifetime,
That I would always have it . . . forever.
Such a wonderful gift, so beautiful, sweet, and innocent.
A gift that anyone would love, a gift much more precious
Than a young girl could ever know.

I loved the gift so much,
I was just too young to treasure it and
Sometimes I failed to protect it the way I should,
Sometimes the gift took all my time, and patience.
Sometimes I got tired and angry at the gift, and
Sometimes I wondered why you gave the gift
To someone so young.
Surely you could have made a better choice,
Someone much older,
Who would have taken better care of the gift,
Much too precious for a young girl to care for.

Then I lost the gift you gave me,
I only got to keep it for twenty-three years,
Not the lifetime, like I thought I would.
I thought the gift was mine to keep forever,
The time I had the gift was much too short
For I had grown older,
More patient and understanding.

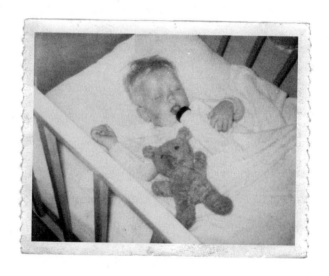

Now you know just how much I learned
To appreciate the gift you gave me, after I lost it,
For I loved it with all my heart.
I know my gift is with you now,
It was never really mine to keep,
I was only supposed to love and care for it,
For a short while.

I'm not that young girl anymore, and
When the time is right
You will give it back to me, and
I will have my child for all eternity.
He will be my gift to love and treasure
Forever and ever.

January 24, 1995

Distance Separates Us

I think about the time that has passed
Since you've been gone,
And I know distance separates us now,
But you're always as close as a thought.
You always live within my heart.

I think of you so many times throughout the day,
And remember all of the special times we had together.
I remember all of the special ways
That you showed that you loved me.
That's something that distance cannot part.

I have all of the wonderful memories that you left me here.
They were short and precious
And were meant to last me a lifetime.
That's all I have of you now,
Are my memories.

I know distance separates us now,
But you will always be a big part of my life,
And live within my heart
Throughout the days, weeks, and years to come.
As the years come and go,
I will be getting closer to you each day,
And the distance will get shorter and shorter.
You'll be waiting for me there.
We'll be together and distance will never separate us again.

January 28, 1995

Mother

TO DR. MARTIN

Many are the memories left behind on this earth,
With the ones we love and know.
We take our memories with us and leave the rest behind,
To help the ones we leave here.
Some of the memories are happy and some are sad.

Only a mother could feel so much love for a child.
God truly knew what he was doing when he made mothers.
We hate to leave our children behind,
But we would rather go a hundred times,
Than to lose a child first.

Things that we wish we had done differently,
For no matter how hard we tried,
It was never really good enough for us.
For we wanted to be perfect,
But it wasn't meant to be,
For we were only mothers,
And God knew, we couldn't be.

Hearts are what we think with, instead of our heads.
A mother's heart is so full of love that sometimes
It breaks with pain for all of the things
We would want to change, but never can.

Each of us has a purpose on this earth.
Some big, some small.
Each of us touches so many lives
As we try to leave something behind.
Each of us will never be forgotten, because we live within
The hearts of the ones we love and leave behind.

Rest awaits us when our job on earth is done.
Keep our many memories and our love
Deep within your hearts,
Overlook our faults, for you know how hard we tried,
And know our love for you will never die.
We will truly be happy, when we meet again.
For God knows a mother's love will never end.

April 30, 1995

If I Had Known Back Then

If I had known back then what I know now
I would change so many things.
I would let you know I'm proud of you
For all the things you tried to do
Your whole life through
No matter how big or small;
I would take this time to see your smile
And really look at you,
For it would be such a short time
For it would have to last me for the rest of my life.

I would have talked to you
Until I could talk no more,
And pray to God to talk some more!
I would try so hard to make your life easier
To make you happy, and to tell you I love you more,
That I wanted you and need you,
If I had known back then what I know now.

I never knew your life would be so short.
I think about all the time I wasted in so many things.
I could have spent this time with you,
Now, oh, what I would give for just a minute or two,
To spend them with you!
I would change so many things if we could just go back;
If I had only known back then what I know now . . .

I took the days with you for granted,
I never truly thanked you for all the things you did for me
To make me love you more,
I never told you how important you were to me.
So many things I left unsaid,
If only I could make them up to you by saying them now.
Pretend this is your last day to tell your loved ones
How much they mean to you.
Live every day as if it were the last, for it could be;
If I had known back then what I know now.

January 20, 1996

I'm Here

I see you every day in all you do
I can see your heart and know it's breaking in two.
I know your pain, I feel it every day.
Wherever you go, I go; I walk with you.
You'll never be alone.
Don't grieve for me, for I'm here.

I see you in the morning light
Your struggles throughout the days,
Weeks, and years that have passed away.
I see all the tears you cry at night
After you turn out your light.
I know that you miss me
And the sorrow breaks your heart in two,
And sometimes you don't know what to do.

I know you feel so sad and all alone.
I let you know every way I can that I'm here.
There won't be a morning or day that ends for you.
I'll be here when you need me.
Look for me in the things I send you every day.
You'll know they're from me and I'm here.
Life is too short to waste it in pain and sorrow.
See me in all you do and keep me alive.
I'll never leave you, I'm here.

My body died, my spirit lives,
Not just today, but every day.
I know your life has never been the same
Since the day I went away.
I'll never be far from you throughout your life,
Every day throughout the weeks and in the coming years
Just know I'm here.

January 20, 1996

Whispers

When I miss you more than I can stand
Or when I don't want to see the world without you in it,
When the pain is just too hard to bear,
You whisper in my ear.
Then I know there is only a fine line that's between us.

When I'm sad and lonely and full of despair
Wishing you were here,
The tears start falling and the break in my heart
Grows larger each day.
When I can't take it any longer
You whisper in my ear.
Then I know the line gets smaller every day.

As the years come and go you never leave my thoughts.
Some would think it would get easier
But the pain is sharp like it was from the start.
Years can never erase the love one feels.
You whisper in my ear.
Then I know you're still here.

One day I'll cross that line that leads to you and keeps us apart.
When we meet again, the pain, loneliness, and sorrow will all fade.
The love and joy will be worth the wait when I see your face.
Until then I'll keep listening to your whispers in my ear.
The whispers that grow louder with each passing year.

June 2, 1996

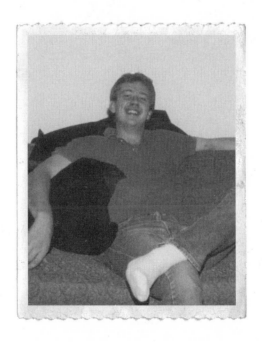

Your Walk in Life

Your walk in life was so short and full of pain,
You searched for joy, but not much came.
You walked roads of broken glass and rocks searching for love.
Rocks and glass so sharp they left scars upon your feet.

The sweat on your brow and tears on your cheeks would run down
But no matter how hard you looked, none could be found.
You worked so hard to do whatever it took;
You searched and searched.
Your mountains were so high they touched the sky,
You swam oceans so deep there was no way, except defeat,
You could never find any love for you.

You tried to get love any way you could.
You struggled and tried to be brave and good.
You walked that road of heartbreak and pain.
You searched and searched for a place to fit,
A place of joy and happiness, a place to be accepted.
A place for a young man searching for love.

Before it was time, your life was taken from you.
All the love you needed, you never found.
God saw your life on earth was not completed
And sometimes the best are the ones who get cheated.
He said, "Come on home, we have all this love just waiting for you,
The hardships, pain, and hurt that you endured are over.
Your search is through, you'll walk the streets of gold
Instead of broken glass and rocks.
Your mountains will be small,
The oceans will soothe you
Our love will surround you.

A perfect place for a young man searching for love,
A place of joy and happiness, a place to fit, a place you belong.
Welcome home, son! Welcome home!"

June 2, 1996

One

I laid me down to rest
For sleep still would not come to me.
With thoughts of you, I said a prayer;
I felt your presence here with me.
I looked up and saw you standing there
No need to speak
For our hearts, minds, and souls were one.

You knew the day you died
My heart and soul were destroyed,
And it seemed that I
Couldn't stand it anymore.
You knew it all,
The sadness, pain, and loss I felt for you.

You saw my heart and soul,
No need to speak out loud.
Our souls are one for now.
You saw the love I have for you.
You were there to comfort me
To give me love and peace.

I saw the happiness you have now
I felt your love for us.
You let me know
All your sadness, hurt, and pain
That happened to you on earth
Were so short and don't matter,
Compared to the way things are now,
For all eternity.

You let me know you are safe,
How much you love and miss us.
You let me know and feel it all,
That we will be together again.
That you will be there,
Waiting and watching over us.

I know you have to leave for now.
You let me know that we will never be alone,
That you are always there,
That our hearts and souls are one forever
Until we're together again.
For time here on earth is short
But eternity is forever.

August 8, 1996

Heavenly Gates

Heavenly gates open wide
And let my precious child inside.
A child who loved others so much in life,
Let those gates open wide.
Let him know he's finally home,
For the one who loves him so
Is waiting there inside.

Heavenly gates welcome him
And let him know his hurt and pain are over,
That there won't be any more tears of sorrow,
Only love and peace inside those heavenly gates.
When it's time for this mother to go
Let her child be waiting for her
Behind those heavenly gates.

Let them swing wide
For that child she loves and longs to see
Is waiting for her inside.
The love she has missed all this time
For a child that she calls "mine."
Heavenly gates open wide
And let my precious child inside.

January 2, 1997

Angel Tears

Their tears were falling from heaven;
They fell upon the ground.
They formed puddles big and round;
They fell for days and days.

They were tears from heaven the night the angels cried,
    You were coming home.
        For God saw your tears and counted every one of them,
      Too many tears for such a short life
        For a child of His.

The night the angels cried, I cried for days and days.
God counted my tears, every one of them,
You were leaving me and going home,
I saw your tears over the years.
Too many for such a short life,
For a child that I called mine.

The night the angels cried, they cried for a child of His
And a child of mine,
Our child was going home.
The night the angels cried I knew I would never be alone,
God counted my tears, every one of them,
You and the angels have dried my tears.
Through all the days, weeks, and years.

December 12, 1997

Heavy Load

Help me carry this heavy load
It's so heavy, God, only you know,
A load so heavy I need you to help me.
I've had to carry it all these years now,
And I know I will never make it without your help.

Help all this pain to end one day
That lives within my heart,
Help all the sorrow to fade away,
So I can live with my broken heart.
Help me to understand why this had to be,
Let me know how to live with so many memories.

Help me live with all the guilt that I live with every day,
That I didn't save this loving child you gave to me,
A child that loved me with all of his heart,
Right from the start.
Help me from always wanting to go back
And change so many things, to do all the right things.
Help me forget that I tried to be perfect,
That my child had to be perfect or he wasn't loved or wanted.
I need you to carry this heavy load for me,
For now I understand no one is perfect,
Not even a mother or a child.

Help me to forgive myself for withholding my love,
Understanding, and sympathy,
And for having a hard heart whenever this child needed me.
Help me carry this heavy load
Until I can be with my child again.
I will deserve him this time. . . .
I had to lose him before I could deserve him,
For I love him with all my heart.

February 20, 1998

A Man You Called Best Friend

There was a man you called best friend,
It was his house you ran to when life let you down.
It was him you trusted, he was the one you talked to.
You were looking for a father or just someone to love you,
This man you called best friend
Now says he hardly knew you.

It made me sad, it broke my heart in two,
How could he do this to you?
Then I remember, a man Jesus called best friend
Denied knowing him too.

Why should you be any different?
You were only the son of a man.
You were just a young man searching for someone to love you,
Someone to care.

Jesus was the son of God, and
He was also searching for someone to love him,
Someone to care.
Two worlds apart, but life ending for the both of you.

A man you called best friend denied knowing you.
Would you be alive today if he had really been your friend?

When we leave this world, will God,
Someone we ran to, talked to, and trusted,
A man we called our best friend, say he hardly knew us?
What will you do if he denies knowing you?

March 20, 1998

A Mother for Life

I think about the years that I had you with me,

Before your life was taken away
On that cold February day.
Too short for a child
When you're a mother for life.

I think about the years that you've been gone from me.

I count them every day.
Too long for a child to be away.
When you're a mother for life.

I think about the years that we'll be together again.

With time slowly passing away,
Too long to wait to see your child
Whom you love and miss so much every day.

Being a mother doesn't end with the death of your child.
For once you're a mother,
You're a mother for life.

July 9, 1998

My Angel

God sent an angel from high up above
He sent him down with all of his love.
He arrived with stars in his eyes,
Oh, how they sparkled, oh, how they shined!

A big smile on his face,
He was so happy to be here with me.
God sent him just for me to love.
You were my angel sent from God above.

God knew I needed him.

After a few short years
The sparkle and shine in his eyes
Had been replaced with tears of pain and sorrow,
The smile had faded away.

The hurt and pain he endured
While he was here with me
Kept tearing away his heart.
So short for me, so long for him.

With broken wings he could not fly
With pain and sorrow.

My angel didn't know where to go,
He never belonged here on this earth.
There were too many scars for my angel to heal.

With his broken wings and shattered heart
God took my angel back.
He could not survive here on earth.
His broken wings have healed now.

His heart has mended, his scars are all gone.

With stars in his eyes,
Oh, how they sparkle, oh, how they shine.
A big smile on his face,

Free from all his pain and sorrow.
He's so happy to be back.
One day I will be with him again,
For God knows I need him.

I'll have my angel back.

August 11, 1998

Christmas in Heaven

Christmas was always your favorite time of year,
You could hardly wait whenever it got near.
You worked so hard for what money you had,
It wasn't much, you spent what you had, it made you very glad
To buy gifts for all those you loved at that time of year,
For you gave with all of your heart.

You've spent Christmas in heaven these past years,
While you were here on earth you saw
So many people you loved who went before you,
And so many you loved since then,
They'll be spending Christmas with you this year.

Your Christmas in heaven is like no other on earth,
Where all the angels sing, the stars are like diamonds
That twinkle, sparkle, and glow,
They cover the heavens wherever you go,
Where you walk on streets of silver and gold,
Much too beautiful for the eye to behold.
You can hardly wait whenever it gets near.

Our Christmas on earth is so hard without you;
Your spirit is here with us always,
As is your love that you send us each day all through the year.
Someday we'll spend Christmas with you and all those we love;
You can hardly wait. The best gift of all is the ones we love,
And for our Christmas in heaven we can hardly wait.

December 4, 1998

Tim and Tony

To Tony Bentley
March 21, 1962, to October 1, 1989

The same blood did not run through their veins,
But they were brothers just the same.

They were always there for each other, after they first met,
They were young and full of life,
They had lots of fun,
They loved the girls who broke their hearts.

Their laughter was like music,
Their smiles would light up the night,
Their ways were sweet and kind,
They were there to help each other along,
Never knowing their lives wouldn't last that long.

The same blood did not run through their veins,
But they were brothers just the same.
Always smiling,
But deep inside they had their pain and sorrow,
Trying hard not to let it show,
Always trying to be strong.

They were brothers in their hearts,
It was meant to be,
Like they had met before,
As if they had known each other all their lives.

Life ended for one,
And eight months later for the other,
Much too young to die,
Before each had a chance to live his life.

They are together now for all eternity,
As if it were meant to be.
The same blood did not run through their veins
But they were brothers just the same.

With their love, smiles, and laughter
They light up the Heavens forever and ever.

March 18, 1999

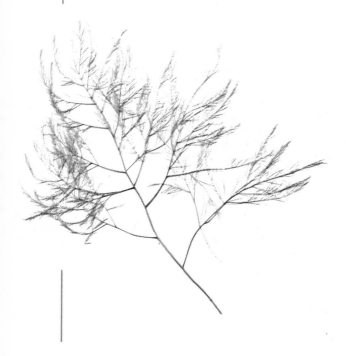

Hear Our Cries

We are victims, hear our cries.
We are the little children of child abuse.
We have been molested, beaten black and blue.

We've been kidnapped,
We've been murdered, too.
We were innocent.

We are children, hear our cries.
We are grandparents, fathers, mothers,
Brothers, sisters, aunts, uncles,
Husbands, and wives.
We have been battered, robbed, raped,
Abused, and murdered.
Hear our cries, for we need your help.

Help us to stop the pain,
For we all will never be the same.

We come from all walks of life.
There are victims every day.
Hear our cries.
We are innocent.
Feel our pain.

We try to fight,
We try to heal,
We are helpless.
Our cries go unheard.

Some of our lives have been destroyed.
The pain is so terrible we cannot exist.
It has torn our hearts and souls apart.

Some of us go on, for it changed our lives.
For we heard the cries,
We felt the pain and sorrow,
We had the loss.

Help our pain, bruises, sorrow,
Our hearts to heal,
Our souls to mend.
Give us hope.
Help the nightmares to end.

Help us to go on to face another day,
Some of us will never be heard.
For our lives have been taken away from us.

Some of us are innocent children,
Too small to speak.

Some of us are old,
Our hearts are weak.

Some of us are afraid to speak out
And some of us have disappeared.
No one knows, no one hears.

We were all someone's loved one.
We are all victims.
Hear our cries.

About the Author

June Keatts Wiggins is the fifth of ten children born to Billy and Annie Keatts in the small town of Indian Mound in Stewart County, Tennessee, and grew up in Dickson County. She enjoys writing, interior decorating, and travel.

Wiggins's eldest son, Tim, died in 1989. She began writing poetry as a means of coping with her unspeakable grief, and her work vividly describes her experiences as a result of the tragic loss of her son.

Since Tim's death, Wiggins has been involved with the Victims' Coalition of Tennessee and the Organized Victims of Violent Crimes, two organizations that work to promote victims' rights as they struggle for truth and justice. Both organizations speak on behalf of victims and their families and work to ensure the passage of legislation to protect victims' rights.

The recipient of numerous awards for her writing, Wiggins now resides in Nashville, Tennessee, with her husband, Tom.